**Forming Family Core Values,
A Mission Statement, Goals, and
Strong Family Traditions**

by

Jennifer Daly

Written by: Jennifer Daly

House United Publishing ©2022

All rights reserved.

ISBN: 978-1-7376487-1-0

Thank you for picking up this book and investing in your family. Strong families make strong communities and now, more than ever, we need to come together!

Dedicated to Team Daly, your family, and many more… keep loving, serving, and cheering others on. Thank you for your support.

CONTENTS

WHY?

SESSION 1: FAMILY DISCUSSIONS

SESSION 2: CORE VALUES

SESSION 3: FAMILY GOALS

SESSION 4: MISSION STATEMENT

SESSION 5: FAMILY TRADITIONS

family

WHY?

Thank you for being a family willing to step up and fight the good fight. Everything in this world tells you that the institution of the family doesn't matter. But I'm here to tell you that you matter, your actions matter, and the legacy of your family is eternal.

We tend to get so busy in our day-to-day that the little moments that matter, escape our attention. The opportunity to kneel down and make eye contact with our littles, hold their hands, and listen to their stories are often erased with our half attention on them while holding a phone and keeping our life in an ever-constant state of motion. Can you relate? I know I can. I can feel it sometimes hit me as my youngest walks away and I can't remember what she just said. Sometimes, I look at my oldest and think, how did we get here so quickly? Realizing that I've had more time with her already than the time she has left at home. I can't help but look at her and think, have I helped her enough? Have I given her the right tools? Have I modeled a life of loving God and serving others? That is the core of whom I want my children to be but am I thinking it and not modeling it?

I came to the realization that while my husband Daniel, and I talk about what is right and wrong, and we've tried to model who we are as a family and what's important to us, I know we've never actually discussed it as a family.

Friend, now is always the right time to invest in your family and future. As Daniel and I began formulating a plan and guide to building our family foundations, I knew others could benefit from this too.

As you begin this journey together, I encourage you to decide the when, where, and frequency of how you will complete this book. Having a game plan is essential. We all start books with the best of intentions but how often have you been disappointed in your unfinished results? This is too important! Your family deserves your attention. Make the plans, show up and finish strong. After you've mapped out your plan on the next page, set this book down and put the five sessions in your calendar. And I'm saying this with a smile, knowing your five sessions away from a firm family foundation.

When we will do our family sessions:

Family Discussions:

Core Values:

Family Goals:

Mission Statement:

Family Traditions:

SESSION 1: FAMILY DISCUSSIONS

Use the following spaces to answer the questions as a family. Be honest with one another and allow the discussions to go off track but, eventually, reroute them back to answer the question. If sitting down as a family and answering the questions doesn't seem like a possible reality then ask these questions at random times as conversation starters at the breakfast table, in the car, etc. If you have younger children that are not ready for these types of conversations then please take the time with your spouse to answer them. When your children are old enough, go through this book with them and it will be fun to see how your family dynamic has changed!

Part of answering the questions is bringing your own interpretation to them. Each family is unique so use the questions as a baseline then dive off and have fun!

1) Every family member, please state at least one thing you **love** about our family.

2) What city best represents the style of our family and why? (Are we slow-paced like a small town or fast-paced like New York City?)

3) Are we dog or cat people?

4) What does our family name mean? (Do we know the history of our name? Does it stand for something from the past?)

5) What are three things we don't compromise on?

6) Are we a beach or mountain family?

7) What are our family rules? Do we know them or are they unspoken?

8) What is important to our family?

9) What do we like to do for fun?

10) What are some things we want in the future as a family?

11) When other people see our family, what do you think they think? Are they right?

12) For fun, each family member gets to makeup and ask their own questions.

SESSION 2: CORE VALUES

Core Values are considered to be what your family values the most. They are at the core and foundation of your family. Talk with each other about what you believe you are currently demonstrating as your family core values. Are they spoken or unspoken? You may even find that you have some signs or plaques in your home that state your values. Core values are those traits that you center your lives around that are not spoken but may be seen through action. Examples include faith, kindness, generosity, honesty, integrity, respect, compassion, communication, courage, empathy, and teamwork.

1) What are some of our unspoken core values?

2) What are some core values we want to have and show each other?

3) Agree on at least three and no more than six family core values. This is an important time to discuss, hear each other out, reflect and then come together on your core values. Use the next page for your formalized list.

Our Family Core Values:

SESSION 3: FAMILY GOALS

Do you have an idea of where you'd like to see your family in five or ten years? We often have these images and visions for the future in our heads but never discuss them with one another.

For me, I want my girls to come back from college, and years beyond, to visit us often. One day I hope to have grandchildren who live nearby. But I have to ask myself, am I working towards making that a reality? Do my girls know I have these goals? What if their goals include moving far away after school? Or visiting countries around the globe for a few years?

I believe it's important for our children to know we have a vision for the future. We also need to share that we're imperfect and some goals we set may not always happen as we envision. Share with your children some personal goals you've set in the past that didn't go according to plan. Were you glad you set the goal? Did you grow and learn from the outcome?

It's important to be flexible and realistic with our visions for the future. Starting with a plan is always a great idea. We would never get in a car and just start driving, hoping we end up where we want to go. Why do that with our families? Let's get in alignment and collectively set a vision for where we want to head as a family.

1) Discuss some of your personal goals and provide tangible end results.

2) Every family member take a turn and offer one to three family goals. Examples include: vacationing twice a year, taking an international trip, saving money for a pool or major house renovation, purchasing a family fun vehicle, taking a quick weekend getaway every other month, eating better, everyone taking turns cooking, sharing family chores, get outside more, etc.

3) Write out at least three to five family future goals.

   a) Put a timeframe on them. For example, want to take a big family trip twice a year? Great! When will we do this?

   b) Please include concrete examples as, if you want to eat healthier as a family, what does that mean? Are you cutting out fried foods together? For how long?

Every great goal can only be achieved when you make a plan for it to happen. So use the space below to not only write out your goals (pick at least three above) but the details of when and how.

Our Family Goals
(with your when and how details)

Family Goal and Timeline 1:

Family Goal and Timeline 2:

Family Goal and Timeline 3:

Family Goal and Timeline 4:

Family Goal and Timeline 5:

SESSION 4: MISSION STATEMENT

Now that you've had some family discussions and brainstorming sessions, it's now time to begin crafting your family mission statement. Consider your goals, your hopes, and your family core values. Begin to discuss how you might summarize all of those thoughts. What would that sentence be?

A family mission statement entails your purpose, your impact, and your joint mission. This will take some more discussion, some editing, some tweaking, possibly even coffee for some family members. You may need to walk away and then come back to make a statement you're all happy with.

Although challenging at times, these discussions are meant to bring your family closer together. They are meant to help you navigate those conversions that may be difficult to have. But continue to persevere. Don't give up and you'll be truly joyful over the outcome and finished product!

Family Mission Statement Example: Team Daly exists to bring glory to God by authentically loving and serving others, being generous with our time and talents, and being kind communicators.

Use the space below to brainstorm and then the following page to write out your Family Mission Statement.

Our Family Mission Statement:

SESSION 5: FAMILY TRADITIONS

Are you ready to have some fun? You've made it through the challenging work and now we get to talk about your fun traditions; those things you do that make your family unique!

Examples of family traditions: Going to the beach every summer, collecting Christmas ornaments while on vacation, spending Christmas Eve with the in-laws, spring break getaways, taking a mother/daughter weekend each fall, or always going to Grandma's house for Thanksgiving.

Sometimes traditions happen by accident and those can be some of the best memories made! While in high school, I unwrapped a present at Christmastime only to find I had been gifted an empty box! Our family laughed so hard when we realized my Grandma had accidentally wrapped a box she thought she had put a present in! This made such an impression we have kept the Christmas tradition going, and now we wait to see each year who gets the empty box. My girls have both been gifted an empty box and I'm sure they will pass on this fun "tradition" when they have families of their own! Have you had something similar where your family created an "accidental" tradition?

Whether you already have a list of fun traditions, or you are ready to start making some new ones, follow these prompts to get your ideas flowing. Remember, this is all about having fun!

Things we consistently do as a family:

During a specific time or place (think holidays, weekends, seasonal events, etc.)

In general:

Things we would like to do as family traditions:

Our Family Traditions:

Our Family Foundations - Instructions

Now it's time to take everything you've been working on and put it on one page. Once you've got that done, then you can print, frame and hang it up. Place it somewhere everyone in the family will be able to see, enjoy and remember your team effort creating your family foundations. Please use all of this space to work for additional brainstorming, if needed, so the next page is nothing but your final draft. Have fun! Be creative and make it look just as unique as your family!

Our Family Foundations

Our Family Core Values:

Our Family Goals:

Our Family Mission Statement:

Our Family Traditions:

Bonus Content

Bonus 1 - Prayers for our family

For Team Daly, faith is the core of our family foundation so I've included some faith-based bonus materials that are meant to further strengthen and serve your family well.

Using the space below, write out prayers for your family that you can pray both individually and as a team, long term. Discuss them and share why you would use the words you've chosen and what they mean to you.

For example, "Lord, thank you for our family. May you lead and guide us today and each day to follow your will and shine your light."

Our family prayers:

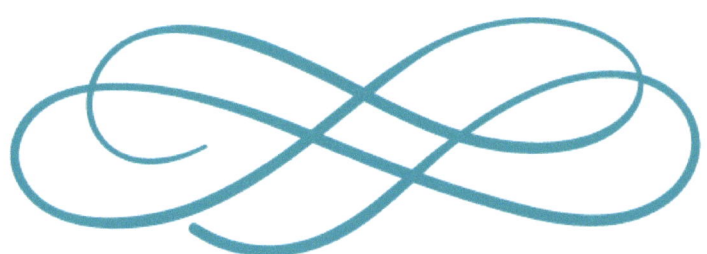

Bonus 2 - Our Family Verses

Have you ever read a verse that speaks to you? It's as if God was speaking those very words directly to you. Or maybe you've read a verse that was very applicable in the moment. It was exactly what you needed to hear at that time. Use the space below to write out verses that have spoken peace, blessings, and/or wisdom to you and your family in the past. Then, use the additional space for verses you'd like to hold onto for your family's future.

Verses that have helped our family:

Verses for the future of our family:

Bonus 3 - Verses to Pray Over your Family

These are just a few of the verses we use in our family prayers. As you read your Bible, God will reveal verses that are meaningful for your family and your season of life. Write those down, pray them and insert your family name into them.

Example:

"For I know the plans I have for the Daly family. Plans not to harm you but to give you a future." Jeremiah 29:11 NLT

Other verses to pray over your family, whether you're together or apart:

"May the Lord bless you and protect you. May the Lord smile on you and be gracious to you. May the Lord show you his favor and give you his peace." Numbers 6:24-26 NLT

"And become useful and helpful and kind to one another, tenderhearted (compassionate, understanding, loving-hearted), forgiving one another [readily and freely], as God in Christ forgave you." Ephesians 4:32 AMPC

"My flesh and my heart fail; *But* God *is* the strength of my heart and my portion forever." Psalm 73:26 (NKJV)

"I know the Lord is always with me. I will not be shaken, for He is right beside me." Psalms 16:8 NLT

"I pray that God, the source of hope, will fill you completely with joy and peace because you trust in him. Then you will overflow with confident hope through the power of the Holy Spirit." Romans 15:13 NLT

"Do not let any unwholesome talk come out of your mouths, but only what is helpful for building others up according to their needs, that it may benefit those who listen." Ephesians 4:29 NIV

"As for me and my household, we will serve the LORD." Joshua 24:15 NLV

"These commandments that I give you today are to be upon your hearts. Impress them on your children. Talk about them when you sit at home and when you walk along the road, when you lie down and when you get up." Deuteronomy 6:6-7 NLV

"I pray that you may enjoy good health and that all may go well with you, even as your soul is getting along well." 3 John 1:2 NLT

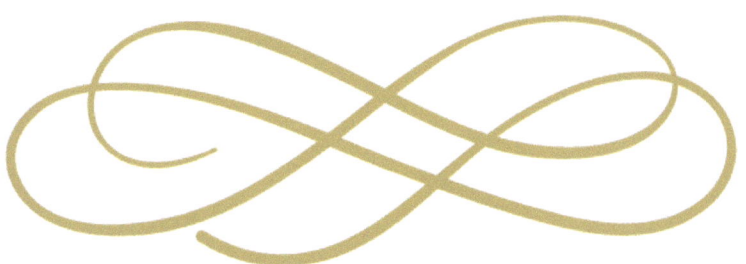

Family Notes:

Thank you again for choosing this book to assist you with your family foundations. I know it was challenging and you really had to dig but that is where the gold can be found! Be sure to store this book somewhere where all family members can see it and remember what you are building together.

About the Author

Jennifer Daly, MBA, PHR, SHRM-CP, lives in the Dallas, Texas area with her hot fire-fighter husband Daniel, her two daughters Zoey and Lexi who light up their lives, and their perfect hairy, German Shepherd, Duke.

Jennifer is the founder of CheeringOnMoms.com where she helps Moms get over the guilt to go after their dreams. Walking the talk, she is a goal-getter, author, speaker, certified life coach, and multi-title holding pageant Queen.